GW00775610

CLEANING AND RESTORING COINS AND ARTEFACTS

Michael J. Cuddeford

Mount Publications

Produced and published by Mount Publications.

© *M.J. Cuddeford 1995*

ISBN   1 900571 00 5

Mount Publications,
PO Box 1916,
Chelmsford,
Essex.
CM3 1EY.

CONTENTS

Introduction   4

1   Cleaning Objects - Methods and
    Equipment   6

2   Restoration and Conservation   11

3   Gold and its Alloys   17

4   Silver and its Alloys   18

5   Copper and its Alloys   21

6   Lead and Tin Alloys   26

7   Iron and its Alloys   27

8   Health and Safety   30

Appendix 1 Summary of substances   *32*

Appendix 2 Summary of equipment   *34*

Appendix 3 Volumes, weights and measures   *37*

Further Reading   *38*

Suppliers   *39*

INTRODUCTION

The full title of this book should more correctly be "Cleaning, Restoring, Conserving and Making Replicas of Coins and other Metal Artefacts", but that would have been a little long-winded. It is however the essence of what this book covers, with non-metallic collectables being excluded, and restoration and conservation dealt with, in addition to details of how to make cast metal replicas of objects.

Open any book on collecting and almost without exception, if mention is made of cleaning coins and artefacts, you will be advised not to. This book does the opposite! The reason why most writers advise against cleaning is simply that it is so easy to ruin things, and so it is safer to say don't, and leave it to the experts. And I am not disagreeing with this. If an object seems to have any significant historical or monetary value, and if you are not totally confident that you are competent to successfully improve it, then the same advice holds good. Either leave it alone, or consult an expert.

But there still remains a large area of possibility for the amateur to undertake his or her own restoration, and sometimes with highly profitable results. Coins and artefacts are regularly recovered by metal detector users, and virtually all require some degree of cleaning and conservation. In addition, it is frequently possible to buy job lots of low grade coins and artefacts from dealers or through auction, and with some careful work multiply their resale value many times over. This is generally due to the fact that it is not economical for a dealer to spend many hours cleaning low grade items, when he could be making more money by trading better quality ones. As a result, for anyone with patience enough to do it, many saleable coins and artefacts can be trawled from the inevitably large number which are beyond improvement. I once purchased a job lot of several hundred encrusted bronze coins from a street trader in the Middle East. After haggling , I paid about the equivalent of £5 for the lot. Following several weeks of careful cleaning, I had a couple of hundred worn and corroded coins of little value, but enough collectable ones to pay for my entire trip! Not only were there some really nice Greek and Roman bronze coins, but several quite valuable silver ones as well, yet until cleaning they had all looked like low-grade bronzes under their encrustation.

The subject of cleaning and conservation has always seemed a rather daunting one to most laymen. The few books published on the subject tend to be fairly technical, and many of the chemicals mentioned are of a hazardous nature, and are difficult to obtain in small quantities by private individuals. This book aims to remedy that situation to some degree, by providing details of some of the more basic cleaning and conservation methods, and by listing specialist suppliers who can provide for amateur needs.

As far as hazardous substances go, some of the most dangerous have been deliberately omitted. There are for example professional conservators and restorers of ancient metalwork who have their own 'secret recipes' for achieving remarkable results, but some of these involve the use of concentrated acids capable of doing considerable damage to flesh and blood. Certainly some substances included in this book are toxic and potentially hazardous, but then so are many everyday domestic products. No one would deliberately drink household bleach any more than they would benzotriazole, nor smoke over a can of petrol any more than a beaker of acetone. At the back of this book can be found a complete list of all chemicals and materials mentioned in the text, together with their health and safety requirements, which should be read and understood.

What I do not advocate is that anyone should rush out and go straight into cleaning coins and artefacts without first fully understanding the processes covered in this book. Only when you have experimented on numerous objects known to have no value should you contemplate moving on to more ambitious projects. Continual success in cleaning and conservation comes with long experience, and even then failures will occur. There are certain circumstances where the eye alone will guide you on how to best tackle a particular problem, and there will be no clear textbook answer. The golden rule is, if in doubt don't! But with care and patience, there is no reason why most people cannot tackle general conservation tasks, and I hope you will find this book of help.

Michael J. Cuddeford.

1

Cleaning Objects - Methods and Equipment

To clean, or not to clean? The answer depends on what an object is, what it looks like, and what it is hoped it might be made to look like. Common preferences will be covered more fully in the sections dealing with specific metals, but in general the only point in cleaning an object is to improve its visual appearance, or to better prepare it for conservation. If something looks OK, and is stable, then it is best left alone.

Cleaning may be desired in cases where something is unevenly patinated, where detail is obscured by encrustation, or where ongoing deterioration is evident. Corrosion on metal is the result of chemical reactions, which can occur when metal objects are buried or exposed to the air. In some cases it can enhance the appearance of an object and increase its value, whilst in others it will detract from it. In its mildest form, corrosion involves nothing more than a change of surface colour, where it might be referred to as tarnish or light patination. In such cases the metal surface below can be restored by the application of a suitable cleaner and polishing. Heavier patination can involve the replacement of a metal object's surface with metal salts. This is common with bronze objects, and when hard and even often produces a desirable surface coloration. Frequently, if this is removed, the underlying surface will be pitted and most unattractive. With more advanced decay, the metal content of an entire object may be replaced by corrosion products. Again, this may be even and follow the shape of the original object, or it may be distorted and 'warty'. Iron is a good example of how corrosion, rust, can go from a light discolouration to a misshaped mass in a relatively short space of time.

The first step in any cleaning operation is to assess as accurately as possible the extent of corrosion and how much if any needs to be removed, and then to try and visualise the appearance of the object once cleaned. This can be established by examination, or by detaching a small part of any encrustation to see the extent of sound metal. Some metals are plated or have enamel inlays, and these will also have to be taken into account. Professionals sometimes use X-rays to assist in this. Having established as far as possible the nature of the corrosion and the condition of the underlying object, and with an end result visualised, one or several of the following methods may be used.

Mechanical Cleaning

This involves the removal of surface deposits by hand. Loose powdery deposits can be removed by brushing. A selection of toothbrushes with different levels of bristle hardness are useful. Another type of brush that produces good results is a typeface brush of the sort used to clean typewriters. Except for cleaning large iron objects, wire brushes should be avoided as they produce a harsh finish. Brass suede brushes also deposit a thin film of brass on metal, further ruining the appearance. Glass fibre bristle brushes are useful for small areas of deposit. Corrosion products of medium hardness can be reduced by cutting away with a scalpel. Hard areas of deposit can be removed by picking off with a sharp instrument. Very fine work can be carried out using an ordinary sewing needle, held either in a pair of pincers, or fixed into a suitable holder. By far the most manageable implements are dental picks of the type used for removing plaque from teeth. These can also be modified by grinding the ends into sharp points or chisel points. Corrosion is removed by direct downwards pressure, causing small pieces of encrustation to detach bit by bit. It is important to maintain direct vertical pressure, and to work in from the edge of an area of corrosion. Starting in the middle of an area, or using an implement at an angle, could cause a brittle object to fracture. Large areas can be cleaned in this way, although it is by necessity a slow process, and care must be taken not to pit the underlying metal. The different configurations of dental pick point also allow for scraping deposits out of awkward corners. Wooden probes such as toothpicks or cocktail sticks are used for removing softer deposits overlying delicate surfaces. A bench-mounted magnifying glass is a useful accessory for fine detailed work.

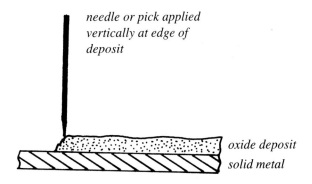

needle or pick applied vertically at edge of deposit

oxide deposit
solid metal

Correct method for mechanical removal of corrosion deposits

There are two types of hobbyist power tool which are invaluable aids to cleaning metal objects. These are small hand held power drills, and engraving tools. The power drills come with a range of small grinders and cutters which greatly assist in the reduction of large areas of deposit, leaving much less to be removed by careful hand picking. Engraving tools that operate with a vibrating rather than rotating action are used in the same way as applying downwards hand pressure, but provide both controllable power together with more rapid coverage. It is necessary to modify some of the bits provided by adapting a needle. A hole is drilled in a suitable bit, a needle inserted and then securely soldered. The point of the needle must be snipped off and safely disposed of, and the resulting end ground to a fine chisel point. This can be used to remove small flakes of encrustation, either with direct pressure, or by undercutting.

Barrelling Machines

These are adaptations of gemstone polishing machines, and consist of a plastic drum which is filled with abrasive material together with the objects to be polished. They are used for bulk cleaning of certain types of metal find. For this purpose, they are partially filled with small steel 'shapes' in a soap solution. Objects to be cleaned are then added and the drum is rotated for a period of time. This is a very harsh method and is generally only used for solid copper-alloy objects such as recent coinage, or modern badges etc. With practice, the results are fairly controllable, and different finishes can be achieved. These can range from a semi-matt finish on copper coins to a bright metal finish on brass army badges. Extended use can over-polish objects and leave them with an eroded appearance. They should not be used on any object that has been plated or enamelled, as this will also be removed.

Barrelling Machine

Electrolytic Cleaning

For cleaning purposes, electrolytic or electrolysis cleaning is a reversal of the electroplating method. Instead of depositing metal on an object, by reversing the polarity, surface coating is removed. The equipment consists of a transformer and two electrodes (- cathode and + anode). The 'business end' of the anode is usually a stainless steel rod, and the cathode a clip or wire frame which holds the object to be cleaned. These are placed in a glass or plastic container, to which is added a solution called the electrolyte. This will normally be water plus a small amount of table salt and a suitable cleaning agent, typically caustic soda or citric acid. A current is then passed through and the surface coating of the object to be cleaned will start to detach. If left this will eventually strip the object down to bare metal, which is rarely desirable, but the method can also be employed to soften or remove part of the deposit to allow hand finishing.

Localised electrolytic cleaning is also possible. This may be employed to remove odd spots of stubborn corrosion. The object to be cleaned remains connected as the cathode, but a probe is substituted for the anode, and, using a damp swab of electrolyte, this can be touched onto the area needing to be cleaned, leaving the rest of the object unaffected.

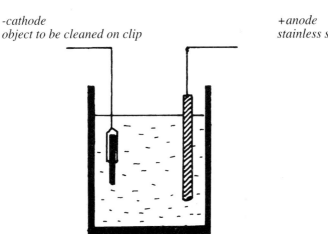

-cathode
object to be cleaned on clip

+anode
stainless steel rod

electrolytic cleaning

Electrochemical Cleaning

This is another form of electrolytic cleaning, in this case creating a chemical reaction without the use of an external electricity source. The process is however essentially the same. The object to be cleaned is placed in a container, to which is added another reagent metal in a suitable solution. This will commonly be zinc and caustic soda, or aluminium and sodium carbonate, depending on what is to be cleaned. The resulting reaction causes the release of hydrogen, which is what effects the cleaning process. This can also be applied directly without the use of a solution in a container (for example cleaning silver coins).

Chemical Cleaning

This involves placing an object to be cleaned in a solution of a suitable chemical, which may be either acid or alkali, and which then dissolves the corrosion products. The stronger the chemical the faster, and consequently less controllable, the process will be.

Miscellaneous Equipment

In addition to the items mentioned, there is a whole range of tools and utensils which will be found useful in cleaning and conservation. A full summary of these can be found in Appendix 2. To elaborate here on some of them, you will need a good supply of rags for general mopping up, wiping and drying. Eye protectors, gloves and face masks are also essential when using corrosive liquids, when there is a risk of inhaling dust, or when engaged in mechanical cleaning. A number of containers will be required for use as baths for the immersion of objects in chemicals. Typically, plastic food storage containers of the sort sold in supermarkets or hardware stores can be used, although old ice-cream boxes are also quite adequate. Plastic bottles with screw stoppers are useful for storing cleaning solutions which . have been made up from solids. Some, like BTA or EDTA, can be reused a number of times and so need to be stored in between applications. Proper laboratory bottles are best, but again quite adequate ones can be purchased through domestic outlets, or domestic product containers thoroughly washed and reused. Some form of heat resistant container will also be required. Some chemicals such as caustic soda generate heat when mixed, and so should not be placed in ordinary glass vessels. Some treatments also require solutions or wax to be heated, and so a suitable container must be employed. Here also domestic cooking equipment can be utilised (but not used for cooking as well!).

2.

Restoration and Conservation

Just as the need to clean an object should be questioned, so should the need to restore it. Restoration usually means replacing something lost, or straightening something bent out of shape. But if that which is replaced is only guessed at, or if being bent is part of an object's history, then it is best left alone.

It is not uncommon for ancient rings to occur that have lost their gemstones. It is of course tempting to replace them with another, either modern or genuinely ancient, but ethically at any rate this should be avoided, as you are creating something that never existed in the first place. You can never know what type of stone was used, or how it was engraved, if at all. In effect the resulting ring is a forgery. Another point to consider is deliberate damage to some types of artefact. In ancient times certain objects, particularly swords and other weapons, were thought to have their own spirits. Just as Japanese swordsmiths forged their blades with religious ritual, so may the ancients have done. Sometimes swords and other valuables were offered to the gods by throwing them into rivers or swamps, or were buried with the dead, and on these occasions they were sometimes deliberately bent out of shape. It is thought that this was a way of ritually 'killing' them so as they would remain with the departed warrior, or perhaps if offerings to the gods they would be rendered useless to the less pious who might seek to retrieve them for their own use. Another type of deliberate damage is the bending of a coin into an 's' shape as a love token. This seems to have been a common practice in the 18th and 19th centuries, with old and worn sixpences being a popular coin for the purpose. To straighten out such a coin is to destroy it as an artefact.

Straightening Bent Artefacts

If it is thought necessary to straighten a bent object, the procedures are fairly basic, although they require some practice. Very few metals that have been bent out of shape can be bent back cold without causing them to break. This is because most manufactured metal objects have a microscopic structure consisting of individual grains. With alloys these will be of different metals, and may have additional impurities incorporated during the original manufacturing process, or as a result of subsequent corrosion. When a metal object is bent these grains are stressed. Further bending causes further stressing and the result is that the object breaks. This is simply demonstrated by picking up any thin strip of metal, and bending it to and fro. Stress cracks quickly appear, and the object finally breaks. The more a metal object is bent, the greater the stressing of the granular structure, and the more likely it will be to break if an attempt is made to straighten it. There is no way of knowing the degree of stressing that a bent object may have been subjected to in the past. In addition, different metals have different structures, and some are more malleable than others.

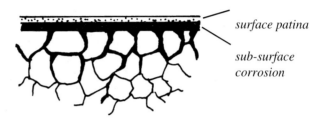

surface patina

sub-surface corrosion

Diagram of metal grains - here sub-surface corrosion is already penetrating deeper.

Judging what may be straightened cold is a matter of experience. Lead objects can sometimes be unbent cold from extreme angles, but silver or copper-alloy objects will very likely break. If the angle of bend is not too severe, thin section objects can often be straightened by placing them between two thin slats of wood or plastic, or by wrapping them in leather or chamois, and then applying pressure either in a vice, or by using a pair of pliers. If after straightening there are still crinkles, more direct pressure can be brought to bear by using thin-nosed pliers. Where small dents are present, these can be pushed out using a wooden dowel in a vice.

Less malleable metals with high melting points have to be straightened by annealing. In this process, the object to be straightened is held in a flame until cherry red, and then plunged into cold water. The effect of this is to de-stress the metal to enable the object to be re-bent. It is frequently necessary to repeat the process, maybe several times if an object has been bent through an extreme angle. But by repeating the annealing process, and straightening a little at a time, it is usually possible to bring an object back to the desired shape.

Having achieved this it is usually necessary to undo some of the damage caused by heating. This can range from discoloration of the surface, to pitting where the heating has burned out corrosion products. Cleaning can be carried out using any of the methods previously described, although it may also be necessary to introduce some form of artificial toning.

NB. Any object with an appreciable potential value should be entrusted to a professional restorer. There is no substitute for years of training and experience, and money spent on a coin or artefact in this way can be recovered many times over at resale by employing such skills.

Polishing out Scratches

This primarily applies to gold and silver, gold in particular being susceptible to damage. Deep cuts and gouges are difficult to remove and are best left. Minor abrasions however can be polished out. Fine grade emery paper wrapped around the end of a wooden toothpick can be used for initial polishing. The emery paper should be of the 'wet and dry' type and should be used wet. This will remove the worst of any scratch, but will itself leave a mass of tiny scratches. These in turn should be removed by polishing with a little jewellers' rouge, or kitchen scouring cream, on the end of a cotton bud. Polishing is done in a rotary action to blend in any tiny abrasions. Finishing can be done using a hobbyist's drill fitted with a soft buffing head. Polishing out scratches will leave the area of metal looking bright, and it may be necessary to clean and re-tone the whole object. Therefore the overall advantage of polishing out scratches should be carefully considered first.

Patinating Cleaned Objects

A even patina on an ancient object is generally regarded as desirable. Where it is necessary to strip objects to bare metal in the course of cleaning them of encrustation, there are a number of methods available to give them a more acceptable tone. Individual treatments will be covered under the specific metal types, but methods in general involve immersing an object in a suitable chemical, monitoring the reaction, and then removing and washing the object. It may then be necessary to conserve it, and to apply a protective coating. In the case of objects with powdery or unevenly coloured patinas, it is sometimes possible to enhance this by the application of wax or lacquer to improve the appearance and bring out detail.

Conservation Treatments

Buried metal objects tend to corrode at a steady rate, and will either decay completely with all the metal being replaced by corrosion products, or they will stabilise after a period of time. The majority of excavated objects will have only partial corrosion evident, and in a majority of cases can be simply washed, brushed and left alone. In other cases, and particularly where chemical cleaning has been involved, it will be necessary to treat the object to prevent further decay, which can be very rapid once it has had its stability altered. Some iron objects can literally disintegrate in a few days if excavated and left untreated. It is rarely possible to know quite how the chemistry of an object has altered by either exposure to the air or by cleaning, and it is preferable to undertake conservation as soon as possible, rather than to try and arrest an outbreak of decay at a later stage. Conservation methods vary from metal to metal, but normally involve immersion in chemicals followed by the application of a protective coating.

Storage of Objects

It is common to display collectables in wooden cases, and to store coins in wooden cabinets or in plastic envelopes, but the type of material is of importance. Some woods exude resinous vapours, and can form deposits on stored objects. Various plastics and even certain types of paper contain acids which can harm stored objects over a period of time. For this reason there are proprietary storage systems available to collectors which are advertised as being free of harmful substances. If producing display cabinets at home, it is best to use mahogany, and to avoid laminates which may include resinous woods or glues. Airborne moisture is one of the main catalysts which can trigger off corrosion. For this reason it pays to keep a good supply of silica gel bags in and around stored material. Bulk storage can be effected by using plastic freezer boxes or re-using ice cream boxes and the like. These have an airtight lid. Objects should be wrapped in plastic self-sealing bags, but with added perforations to prevent any condensation forming. These can then placed in the plastic boxes together with silica gel bags. They should be checked periodically and any change in colour on the silica gel used as a warning that moisture is present. Silica gel can be dried in a gentle heat in a domestic oven and re-used.

Mahogany coin cabinet and plastic collectors trays for storing coins and artefacts

Replicating Objects

Even when objects have been conserved, it pays to avoid handling them too much. This can wear away protective coatings, and even sweat from hands can have a corrosive effect on certain surfaces. One simple answer is to make replicas of metal objects, which provides a way of sharing them with a wider audience without placing an actual coin or artefact at risk. A valuable object kept under lock and key might also be thought too vulnerable to display or hand round, but with a replica that is possible. When ancient coins and objects are unearthed, replicas provide a means for both finder and landowner to share without actually having to have the object. There are also commercial possibilities, and well-produced replicas of coins and antiquities can find a ready market.

To produce cast replicas of coins and artefacts, it is necessary to buy a number of items. These are most easily obtained in kit form from a specialist supplier. The process is fully described in the kit, but basically an object is first cleaned, then placed in a matrix which is half filled with liquid silicone rubber. This has a hardening agent added, and once set, the other half of the object is treated in the same way. This produces a two-piece mould. The two halves are then joined, and a low melting point metal alloy is then poured into the mould. After cooling the mould is separated, resulting in an exact replica of the original object down to the finest detail. Once produced, the moulds can be reused many times over. The casts themselves can be aged by the application of proprietary toning agents, or even gold plated.

Although such replicas will not withstand close scrutiny, they are still very accurate, and it is advisable to mark them to prevent them being mistaken for genuine articles. A small letter punch can be ordered through a good hardware store, the letter 'R' for 'reproduction' being the most appropriate.

Medieval bronze seal and two cast alloy replicas

Obtaining Chemicals and Equipment Mentioned in this Book

Although many of the substances and items of equipment mentioned in this book can be obtained through ordinary shops and commercial outlets, others can only be ordered through specialist suppliers. Some substances are only available in bulk quantities, which may far exceed the requirements of an individual. In such instances it might be possible for a group of interested parties to pool their resources and order from one of the main laboratory equipment suppliers. Local 'Yellow Pages' may also give details of firms that can supply smaller quantities. Appendixes 1 and 2 at the back of this book indicate where specialist suppliers may be required for certain items. The last two pages give details of companies who can supply many of the items or services mentioned. Alec Tiranti stock a wide range of equipment including scalpels, dental picks, drills and metal colouring fluids. In addition they can supply complete kits for making cast metal replicas of coins and artefacts. Barry Sherlock will undertake the restoration of ancient precious metal artefacts and jewellery, and George Farmer Ltd. can supply engraving tools of the type illustrated below. See their advertisements for further details.

*Engraving tool and hobbyists' drill, with a selection of
bits suitable for cleaning work.*

3.

Gold and its Alloys

Pure gold is rarely used for the manufacture of coins or artefacts. Natural gold sometimes has a high silver content, and this is known as electrum. For manufacturing purposes, gold is normally alloyed with either silver or copper, sometimes both, and this produces a much harder-wearing metal that still retains most of the colour of pure gold, which is of course its main attraction. In its pure state, gold is completely resistant to corrosion, and even when alloyed to quite a high degree remains largely unaffected. Modern alloys of gold are given a carat value, which is the proportion of pure gold to added metal. Pure gold is designated 24 carat, 18 carat is 18/24ths pure, and 9 carat 9/24ths.

Cleaning

Due to their corrosion-resistant properties, the majority of ancient gold objects are unearthed as bright as the day they were buried, and the most that needs to be done is to wash them in warm water using a soft bristle toothbrush. Stubborn deposits of soil can be loosened with a wooden cocktail stick or toothpick. Old gold usually develops an attractive slightly matt orange tone, which will be lost if any attempt is made to clean an object with a cleaning fluid and cloth.

Restoring

Gold objects are easily distorted, but if not too severely bent can be reshaped cold. Moderately bent or crinkled objects can be straightened by wrapping them in chamois leather and applying pressure with a pair of pliers. However, any extreme distortion must be dealt with by annealing. Heat the object to be straightened in a flame until cherry red, then quench in water. Repeat with every 20 -30 degrees of bending. Annealing will discolour gold, which can be cleaned in dilute sulphuric acid. It will also destroy any toning, which can however be restored by an expert.

Scratches in gold can be removed by polishing, although this may produce a brighter colour appearance if the gold is ancient and toned.

Conserving

There will generally be no need to undertake conservation of gold unless very debased, in which case the appropriate treatment for the alloy metal will apply.

4.

Silver and its Alloys

Silver is less malleable than gold, and more susceptible to corrosion. Like gold, silver is also often alloyed, usually with copper. Where this alloy is 50% or more it is often referred to as 'billon'. Modern silver used in jewellery is usually 92.5% silver, or 925 parts per thousand, and is often so marked. Silver may occur plated, usually with gold, in which circumstance it is described as silver-gilt, and silver is itself often used for plating base metal such as bronze. Silver artefacts may also on occasion have decorative inlay such as niello, which is normally made from a fusion of silver sulphide.

Cleaning

The commonest corrosion products to be found on silver are silver sulphide, which is a fine black film, and copper carbonate, which leaches out from the base metal to form a green deposit. Less common but more difficult to deal with is 'horn silver'. This is predominately silver chloride, and it usually appears as a grey encrustation on the metal. Depending on what processes have been at work, toned silver may take on various colour hues, which are often considered more desirable than a brightly cleaned object. In general terms silver artefacts are more collectable if they are either bright or with minimal toning, silver coins more collectable (and thus more valuable) with toning.

Copper carbonate can generally be removed by immersion in a 5% solution of either citric or sulphuric acid. Where copper carbonate is present, it is necessary to decide whether this is due to an object being debased with copper, or whether in fact the object is only silver plated. If heavily debased or if plated, immersion in acid can strip and ruin an object. If any doubts exist, test a small area of a coin or object to be treated with a drop of very dilute acid first.

'Horn silver', or silver chloride, is much harder to tackle. This forms as a crust over an object, and may incorporate with the surface, leaving no precise interface between object and corrosion. Careful exploratory testing with a dental pick or needle may reveal the nature of the corrosion. With affected coins scraping the edge will usually reveal if there is a clear interface or not, although this may vary elsewhere on the object. Such deposits can usually be loosened by electrolytic cleaning using caustic soda as the electrolyte. It may then be possible to prise off small area of horn silver either using wooden cocktail sticks, or even by pressure with a thumbnail. Electrochemical means may also be used, using zinc and caustic soda. It is recommended that such treatment should be followed by repeatedly boiling in changes of distilled water, followed by oven drying at 105 degrees C. Do not use electrolytic means if gilding or niello inlay is suspected.

As stated, the dark toning of silver chloride may be regarded as desirable, particularly on silver coins, but only if attractive. Artefacts are sometimes cleaned bright, and even polished, whilst coins are preferred toned, and if brightly cleaned or polished will lose some of their value. An ideal tone on a coin will be a sheen overlying the metal, with the background slightly darker than the high points. Coins from old collections often look like this, for although they may have once been brightly cleaned, the passage of many years has permitted a protective tarnish to build up. But freshly excavated coins are rarely toned in this way, and it may be felt necessary to strip them to bare metal and then re-tone them. This however should never be done to rare or valuable coins without enough experience to predict the outcome.

Light toning can be removed by using a proprietary cleaner such as Silverdip. For more substantial discolouration electrochemical cleaning can be employed. Wrap the object to be cleaned in aluminium foil, and place in a Pyrex container. Add a small amount of sodium carbonate and then pour on boiling water. Leave to bubble for a while and then remove. Some or all of the surface colouring will have migrated to the aluminium foil, and the object can then be washed. Repeat the process to remove more discolouration as required. The surface of the object can be further cleaned by using a proprietary sink scouring cream. Wet the object and gently rub a little scouring cream over the surface using finger and thumb, and then wash off. More drastic results can be achieved by rubbing with the aluminium foil itself, although this can produce scratches.

The same method can be used for coins, but in many cases with some refinement. Small thin hammered coins that have been excavated often display a heavy and sometimes patchy black toning. A simple way of improving this is to wet the coin, and then using thumb and forefinger simply press a piece of aluminium foil onto both sides of the coin. An electrochemical reaction will occur, with the foil becoming hot. A smell of 'bad eggs' may also be noticed - this is the release of hydrogen sulphide gas as a by-product of the reaction taking place. Remove the coin and rub gently with scouring cream. The result should be a toned background with the raised design and lettering bright silver. With very base or billon silver coins, electrochemical cleaning may have little effect. If this is the case then immersion in very weak acid such as lemon juice may remove any offending deposit, but this can also leave a base coin looking more copper than silver.

Restoring

Like gold, pure silver is quite malleable, but this reduces rapidly the more silver is debased. Slightly bent good silver objects can be straightened cold, coins being flattened using the pliers method. More drastic straightening requires annealing, again the process as gold. Great caution is required with base silver objects. Some hammered coins, particularly of the late Saxon period, are very susceptible to becoming brittle. Often the metal will be heavily crystalline, and will fragment if subjected to any drastic treatment. Impurities can be another problem if they are present in the alloy. The effect of heating may be to burn these out leaving a porous and ugly surface.

If it has been found necessary to clean a silver object such as a coin back to a bright finish, it will often be desirable to return the object to a more presentable toned finish. One quick method is to immerse an object in household bleach. This will quickly darken the surface. It is essential to thoroughly degrease the object first, as a fingerprint could become etched in during the process which would then have to be repeated. A disadvantage of using bleach for coins is that the high points, such as the legends, will darken before the background, which is the reverse of what is usually wanted. If a coin is left until completely blackened it can always be re-cleaned using the aluminium foil method, but each time the process is used more wear and abrasion takes place. A more controllable method of toning a silver coin is to use Tourmaline, a proprietary toning fluid. This can be slightly diluted to further slow the process and make it more controllable. The object must first be degreased by immersing it in an acid (not a solvent), and rinsing in water and drying (Avoid finger marks - rubber gloves should be worn). The object is then placed in a solution of Tourmaline where it will begin to darken. This is usually quite a rapid process and so must be monitored, and the object removed and washed as soon as the desired finish is achieved.

Conserving

Good silver will remain stable, base silver may be treated in a similar manner to copper.

16th century silver coin before and after cleaning

5.

Copper and its Alloys

Copper is used for coins and artefacts in either its natural form, or more commonly alloyed with other metals. With tin added it is called bronze, and if the tin content is very high the bronze may be called 'potin'. When zinc is added to copper the alloy is called brass. Lead and other metals may also be added to give slightly different properties or appearances. Some specific mixtures include gun metal, latten, Britannia metal, and Pinchbeck, which imitates gold.

Cleaning

Coins and artefacts that have been buried are usually found with a green surface coloration. This primarily consists of copper carbonate, but the corrosion products may be complex and contain many other chemicals which give a different appearance, and which may cause instability.

An ancient coin or artefact with a smooth green patina is more collectable than a brightly cleaned object. Some ancient objects found in river silts may have a brassy tone, but few collectors are interested in ancient material that has been polished. As far as coins are concerned, although ancient ones are more desirable with a patina, recent ones are not. A rare Victorian penny with either mint lustre or circulation toning would be highly collectable, but an excavated example with a green patina would be almost worthless. Such criteria mean that in most cases cleaning is unnecessary, except where a coin or object is heavily encrusted, and thus the design is obscured, or if it is unstable and requires conservation.

In general, all copper or copper-alloy objects are best cleaned mechanically. Stripping corrosion products using either chemical or electrolytic means can cause unsightly finishes or induce instability leading to further corrosion. It will be necessary to use these methods in some cases, but only as a last resort.

Coins and artefacts with generally even patinas may have odd deposits of further corrosion which can be removed by picking them off with a dental tool, or by grinding them off with an abrasive drill bit. Coins can often be considerably improved by rubbing with an ink eraser, and sometimes this is the only means of identifying worn specimens. This method is particularly effective with copper coins, jettons and tokens. Excavated examples often have an overall matt copper tone with very little detail evident. These can first be brushed to remove any loose powdery material, and then firmly rubbed with a hard grade ink eraser. This works in a similar way to the traditional method of taking a rubbing from a coin using a pencil and piece of paper. What you achieve is the highlighting of the raised parts of the design. The first visual change is a darkening of the copper colour, followed by the appearance of bare metal on the high points, which is often sufficient to allow a coin to be identified.

17th century copper token halfpenny before and after cleaning by rubbing the surface with an ink eraser

Where more substantial corrosion is present, mechanical methods can be a combination of picking with a dental tool, grinding with an abrasive bit, or using an engraving tool with a specially adapted bit to chip away at deposits of corrosion. Great care must be taken not to pit the surface of an object by applying too much downwards pressure, and consideration must be given to possible inlays or enamels that might be present. Copper-alloy objects may also be plated with gold or silver, and this too can be damaged if sufficient care is not taken. With particularly stubborn spots of corrosion, a drop of weak acid can be applied. After being left a little while this is washed off and the now softened or reduced corrosion area can be cleared by continued mechanical means. Areas of iron corrosion deposited on copper-alloys can be dissolved using a localised application of EDTA.

In certain circumstances, a fine deposit may overlie a good surface that could be harmed by mechanical cleaning methods. Such situations particularly apply to plated objects, such as some coins or buttons. The use of acids would generally be too harsh, and could either strip the plating, or leave any exposed base metal looking unsightly. In such circumstances immersion in a solution of sodium hexametaphosphate will usually prove effective. This is a non-corrosive chemical but which has the effect of slowly dissolving calcareous deposits which commonly occur on copper-alloy objects. An object being cleaned should be removed periodically and lightly brushed in fresh water until enough of the deposit has been removed. Sodium hexametaphosphate is particularly useful when deposits overlie a patina, as usually it is possible to achieve a satisfactory result before the patina is affected to any degree. The solution should be at between 5-15%, and gentle warming will speed the reaction. Prolonged immersion in sodium hexametaphosphate however will eventually strip an object down to bare metal.

Where corrosion products form a solid crust that cannot be adequately tackled by mechanical cleaning, electrolytic or electrochemical methods may be used. It must be noted however that these can remove all traces of plating, enamels or inlay, and so should not be used if any of these are suspected. Electrolytic cleaning can be effected by making a 5% solution of citric acid to which is added a pinch of table salt to improve conductivity. The object to be cleaned is then placed in the appropriate holder, the anode inserted, and the current switched on. The object will emit small bubbles and should be periodically checked, washed and brushed to monitor its progress. It may be found preferable to remove the object once some of the deposit has detached, and to finish cleaning by mechanical methods. Electrochemical cleaning is carried out by placing the object in a Pyrex dish and covering it with coarse zinc powder. A 10% solution of caustic soda is then poured over, a stainless steel utensil being used to replace any zinc granules that have been displaced so as the object is completely covered. The reaction may be speeded up by warming. Using this process it is necessary to replace the zinc powder periodically. The object being cleaned should be rinsed and lightly brushed from time to time. The surface deposit will detach progressively. It is recommended that when using this method, the object should be stripped to bare metal as remaining corrosion can harbour chloride traces which may lead to further decay.

Late Saxon strap end cleaned by electrolytic means.
Note the resulting pitted surface.

In both electrolytic and electrochemical reduction methods, copper may plate back onto the article being cleaned, giving it a pinkish colour. Ideally this should be removed as it can harbour harmful chlorides. It can however also provide a preferable finish to a bare and pitted surface resulting from total stripping. If retained it must be conserved as described below, but might also be toned to give a more attractive appearance.

Restoring

With bent objects, thin section copper-alloy items can be reshaped by annealing, but care must be taken not to overheat, as extensive oxidisation will occur and reduce the attractiveness of the object. More substantial copper-alloy objects are best left as found.

Some copper-alloy items may be improved by enhancing the patina. A patina might for example be powdery or rough-textured. This can often be improved by brushing with a typeface brush. If the colour of the patina is thought to be too light, or perhaps having a patina of different shades, then the addition of a coloured wax can be useful. Because chemical additives in commercial products can potentially cause long-term deterioration, they should not be used on important items. Where their use is appropriate, green, brown or black boot polish sparingly applied and then brushed in will give a dark glossy tone. Plain beeswax may also be used with less drastic coloration. Conservation lacquers can also be applied for appearance purposes.

When cleaning has left a copper-alloy object looking bright, it may be thought desirable to restore some form of patina or toning to it. It is possible to produce convincing green patinas, but this is a difficult and chemically hazardous process. Other safer methods rarely produce satisfactory results. The best option if it is felt necessary to 'tone down' bright metal is to use Tourmaline, as described in the section on silver objects. With copper-alloys, degreasing with acid may render objects liable to further deterioration and so conservation will have to follow.

Conserving

Many copper-alloy objects will remain stable when excavated, and will require no particular conservation treatment. The application of waxes or lacquers as mentioned previously may however aid protection as well as improving the appearance of an object.

One of the most destructive threats to copper-alloy objects is a condition known as 'bronze disease'. This can be recognised by small areas of powdery green corrosion which erupts from below the surface of an object. This is caused by the presence of chlorides which were sealed within the corrosion products, and which can become active if the environment of an object is altered. This may also occur when an object has been subjected to chemical or electrolytic cleaning. Once it takes hold, bronze disease is a progressive form of corrosion which, if left unchecked, can totally destroy an affected object.

The only solution is the removal of the affected areas. This can be achieved either by totally stripping an object back to bare metal, with all its attendant disadvantages, or by picking out any small spots with a dental tool or adapted engraving tool. If any trace of bronze disease is left, it will re-occur.

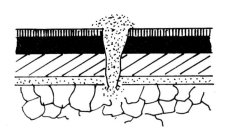

Diagram illustrating 'bronze disease'. Green powdery copper chloride erupts through several different layers of corrosion product. All traces of loose chloride must be removed prior to conservation..

To conserve an object, either following the removal of bronze disease or after any form of cleaning and/or toning, treatment with benzotriazole (BTA for short) is now generally recommended. Before using BTA, an object must first be degreased by immersion in alcohol or acetone. This should then be followed by a week-long soaking in a solution of sodium sesquicarbonate, which will reduce sub-surface chlorides and better prepare an item for treatment.

The next step is to remove the object and allow it to dry, after which it should be placed in a 5% solution of BTA, dissolved in alcohol. It should be left for several days, then removed and once again allowed to dry thoroughly. The final stage is to brush off any loose precipitate that may have formed, and to then apply several coats of a protective lacquer, preferably Incralac or another suitable proprietary conservation lacquer. Domestic varnishes have additives which may be harmful in the long term. The BTA solution can be used repeatedly, and only needs disposing of once it becomes discoloured.

6.

Lead and Tin Alloys

Although quite separate metals, lead and tin were commonly alloyed together to produce pewter, and for the sake of simplicity are grouped together in one section here. Modern pewter is usually made from a lead-free alloy.

Cleaning

Buried lead objects often develop a film of white oxide, which under normal conditions is stable and is best left alone. In some case though, with items such as seals or other objects with lettering or fine detail, the removal of the oxide coating may provide greater legibility. An object to be cleaned should be placed in a 5% solution of EDTA and left until the white oxide coating has dissolved. Tin and pewter objects may exhibit corrosion warts, which in general terms should not be removed. Although the outward appearance of an object might be improved in the short term, removal of warts can cause corrosion to become active. Old pewter may take on a grey or golden patina. This is desirable and should be left. If active corrosion is affecting tin or pewter, then cleaning by electrochemical reduction can be carried out using zinc or aluminium in caustic soda, electrolytic means using caustic soda, or by immersing in EDTA.

Restoring

Lead is very malleable and can usually be straightened at room temperature. However, any corrosion on the site of a bend may be deeply penetrating making an object brittle if an attempt is made to straighten it. Designs or lettering on objects such as seals could be distorted by reshaping. Tin and pewter is likely to be very brittle and in general reshaping is not advisable.

Conserving

Lead and tin alloys that have been cleaned should be coated with a proprietary conservation lacquer.

7.

Iron and its Alloys

Iron used in the manufacture of artefacts is invariably wrought, as opposed to being cast. Cast iron is very brittle and is generally unsuitable for tools. The commonest alloy of iron is steel, which is created by introducing carbon into the production process. Some important weapons or artefacts were produced by forge-welding strips of differently treated metal, and on occassion incorporating steel, particularly where cutting edges were involved. Iron is subject to rapid and drastic decay, and is the most difficult of all artefact metals to stabilise.

Cleaning

The decay processes involving iron can be complex, but in essence rust, or iron oxide, will build up and may ultimately come to completely replace all the metal with corrosion products. In the process an iron object may become heavily distorted with nodules of rust, although internal details such as pattern welding may be preserved, as might the impression of textiles and other organic materials that may have come into contact with an object as it decayed. Such evidence is of value and should not be destroyed. Some iron objects may also have silver or bronze inlay, or include makers marks stamped into them, all of which could be destroyed if not recognised before cleaning. If it is decided to clean an iron object, the method will depend on the substance of the item. Small objects such as arrowheads may have very little original metal remaining, and might be best improved by grinding odd nodules of rust down to conform with the overall shape of the artefact. Solid and undecorated objects such as horseshoes or cannon balls might be subjected to more drastic methods such as chipping off the crust of rust with a hammer and chisel. A heavy crust of oxide can on occasion be loosened by heating an object to red heat first and then quenching it.

Before any cleaning of an iron object is carried out it is necessary to establish how much actual metal remains within the crust. This can be established by testing with a magnet, or by cutting into the crust with a small hacksaw. Mechanical methods are the preferred ones for cleaning iron objects, and light rust can be removed by brushing with a steel brush. More substantial deposits of rust, provided a substantial core remains underneath, might be reduced by grinding, but care must be taken to identify the actual form of the object, and not to grind a shape that did not exist in the first place.

If chemical treatment is thought more appropriate, light rust can be removed by the application of a proprietary cleaning fluid, perhaps aided with the use of wire wool. Heavier rust can be removed by immersion in Biox, a proprietary cleaning substance, which can be used as either a liquid or as a gel. Acids can be used to dissolve oxide crusts, and electrochemical reduction using zinc and caustic soda can be employed, but complete stripping may also severely reduce an object and leave it badly etched.

There are few circumstances in which it will be thought desirable to straighten bent iron objects, the corrosion products usually making them too fragile. Even if reheated in a forge, the resultant surface is likely to be disfigured.

Medieval iron arrowhead after cleaning and conservation. This gave a very weak magnetic reading, and so only had odd lumps of rust removed by hand, and by using a small grinding wheel in a drill. It was then boiled in caustic soda, followed by immersion in microcrystalline wax, and finally coated with Incralac conservation lacquer.

Conserving

Any recently excavated or cleaned iron object must be conserved rapidly, as salts incorporated into the corrosion products can become active once an item is removed from a stable environment. An electrochemical reaction of the same type employed for cleaning may occur within the structure of the object, resulting in rapid disintegration. The first signs of this are 'sweating'. This is the appearance of small droplets of rusty water, which will be followed by the break-up of the object itself. Cracks will appear, followed by the lamination and detachment of sections of an object. This is caused by chlorides within the corrosion products, and these must be neutralised before any deterioration such as 'sweating' becomes evident.

To reduce chlorides, an object must be boiled in a 5% solution of caustic soda dissolved in distilled water, with several changes of solution. This to be followed by repeated boiling in distilled water on its own. This is further followed by thorough drying in a warm oven, with several days subsequent drying in a totally moisture-free environment. Silica gel may be placed by a drying object to absorb any moisture still present. Although boiling will eliminate chlorides in the corrosion products themselves, it may have little effect where chloride deposits form an interface with the actual metal, and so once an iron object is thoroughly dried out, immersion in a solvent such as acetone may help displace remaining chlorides. After this, it must be sealed from any further air contact. One method is to impregnate an object with microcrystalline wax. Place sufficient wax lumps in a suitable container and melt. Then using tongs place the object to be treated into the wax and leave it to simmer with the wax bubbling around it. Under no circumstances cover the pan or the wax may ignite with the same intensity as fat in a chip frier. After an hour or so (adding more wax if necessary) remove the object with tongs or forceps and place onto a suitable receptacle, such as paper towels on a baking tray. It is necessary to melt off surplus wax, which can be done by directing a hair dryer at it. Following this it must be protected with a suitable conservation lacquer. The use of commercial paints is not recommended, as these will obscure the surface details of an object. The best results are obtained with manually cleaned objects impregnated with wax and coated with a clear lacquer

8.

Health and Safety

As explained earlier, although some of the substances and processes mentioned are hazardous, they are no more so than many other domestic applications, and only care and commonsense are needed for successful results. However, it is essential that you fully understand the properties of the materials used, and their attendant dangers. Appendix 1 lists all the chemicals and materials referred to in the book, with full details of their potential hazards, as well as possible sources of supply. This must be read thoroughly.

Handling Chemicals

•   Where chemicals or substances are identified as hazardous, follow any instructions provided with the product. Read all labels carefully. Where appropriate, eye protection, surgical gloves and face masks should be worn. Use stainless steel tongs to place and remove objects in and out of solutions.
•   Never mix substances without knowing what the outcome will be, as volatile reactions or the emission of toxic gases could result. Avoid using concentrated acids. Adding water to acid will cause a volatile reaction.
•   Only use chemicals in a well ventilated area such as a garage or outbuilding. Never use a naked flame near any stored inflammable substance. Ensure work areas are out of the way of children or pets. Take care not to contaminate kitchen worktops or utensils.
•   Keep all substances in manufacturers' own containers or other child-proof containers, out of easy reach in a cool, dark, damp-free location. Ensure all containers are clearly labelled with their contents, never reuse a labelled container for another substance.

Accidents and Spillages

•   Always keep a supply of fresh water to hand. All spillages should be cleared up immediately. If any corrosive substance is spilt on skin the affected area should be held in running water. If any corrosive substance gets into the eyes they should likewise be flushed out with running water immediately, and medical advice sought without delay.

Disposal of Chemicals

• Used substances must never be poured down sinks or drains. This is a major source of pollution. Used substances should be put into sealed containers and placed in a secure refuse receptacle for collection, or taken to a civic amenity point for disposal. One policy is to collect empty plastic bottles such as supermarket milk bottles or similar sealable containers, wash them out and use them for the storage and subsequent disposal of used cleaning substances, which should of course never be mixed. Containers should also be clearly labelled to avoid any confusion with the original product, and kept right away from the domestic environment.

Electrical Equipment and Tools

• If using proprietary electrolytic equipment, ensure that plugs and fuses used are as recommended. Do not attempt to construct your own equipment using domestic electricity supplies or car batteries.
• Wear eye protection when picking off corrosion, or when using drills or engraving tools for corrosion removal.

The author and publishers of this book will accept no liability for any injury or accident, or damage to persons or property, that may arise from the use of any materials or procedures herein described.

Appendix 1

Summary of Substances Mentioned in Text

This list gives details of uses for each substance, health and safety considerations, and sources of supply.

Acetone
Used as a solvent. Highly inflammable. Do not inhale or ingest. Secure ventilated storage required. Specialist supplier.

Alcohol
Used as a solvent. Domestic type such as methylated spirits usable, but industrial type without additives preferable. Domestic or specialist supplier.

Aluminium Foil
Used as reagent metal in electrochemical reduction. Domestic supplier.

Beeswax
Used for patina enhancement. Domestic or specialist supplier.

Benzotriazole (BTA)
Used as a corrosion inhibitor. Possible carcinogen. Protect against eye or skin contact. Wear gloves to handle treated objects until lacquered. Do not inhale or ingest. Specialist supplier.

Biox
Corrosion remover. available as liquid or gel. Specialist supplier.

Caustic Soda (Sodium Hydroxide)
Used as a cleaning agent. Corrosive. Toxic. Protect against eye or skin contact. Only add to water, never pour water over the powder as this can cause a volatile reaction. Use Pyrex vessels only as mixing generates heat. Exercise caution if using boiling solution. Domestic supplier.

Citric Acid
Weak acid used for cleaning. Obtainable as crystals, or as lemon juice or vinegar. Avoid eye contact. Domestic supplier.

Conservation Lacquer
Used for protection and enhancement of metal surfaces. Do not inhale or ingest. Proprietary brand Incralac recommended. Avoid domestic lacquers. Specialist supplier.

Distilled Water
Used for all processes. Preferable to tap water as it contains no impurities. Domestic supplier.

EDTA (Ethylenediaminetetra-acetic acid)
Used as a corrosion remover. Best obtained as disodium salt. Do not inhale or ingest. Protect against eye and skin contact. Specialist supplier.

Jewellers Rouge
Commercial polishing medium. Domestic or specialist supplier.
Microcrystalline Wax
Used for impregnating objects as a corrosion inhibitor. Do not ingest. Inflammable. It will ignite if boiled in a covered pan. Specialist supplier.
Scouring Cream
Household product used for enhancing metal surfaces. Do not ingest. Domestic supplier.
Shoe Polish
Used to enhance patinas on copper-alloys. Do not ingest. Domestic supplier.
Silica Gel
Moisture absorbent. Use in bags. Do not ingest. Usually specialist supplier.
Silicone Rubber
Used for taking accurate casts of objects for replica making. Do not ingest. Specialist supplier.
Silverdip
Proprietary silver cleaning fluid. Do not ingest. Domestic supplier.
Sodium Carbonate (Washing soda)
Used as reagent chemical. Do not ingest. Domestic supplier.
Sodium Hexametaphosphate
Used as a solvent for calcareous deposits. Formerly available as 'Calgon' water softener but no longer included as an ingredient. Do not ingest. Specialist supplier.
Sodium Sesquicarbonate
Used to neutralise acids and to dissolve chlorides. Do not ingest. Specialist supplier.
Sulphuric Acid
Used as a solvent for some metal salts. Corrosive. Protect against eye or skin contact. Do not ingest. Purchase only as 5% or 10% solution. Specialist supplier.
Table Salt (Sodium Chloride)
Used to improve conductivity of electrolyte. Domestic supplier.
Tourmaline
Proprietary metal colouring fluid. Protect against eye or skin contact. Do not ingest. Specialist supplier.
Zinc Powder
Used as a reagent metal in electrochemical cleaning. Do not inhale or ingest.. Obtainable as fine powder, course powder or granules. Course powder most suitable for small objects. Specialist supplier.

Appendix 2

Summary of Equipment Mentioned in the Text

Some additional useful items have been added although not mentioned specifically in the text.

Balance
Used for weighing accurate amounts of solids. Also essential for coin collectors to check for forgeries and to record coins etc. Available as electronic balances weighing to two decimal places of a gram, or more economically as arm balances weighing to one decimal place.

Barrelling Machine
An adaption of a gemstone polisher used for cleaning modern coins etc. Specialist supplier.

Brushes
Various types. Wire brush for iron; different hardness toothbrushes; glass fibre bristle brush; typeface brush; artists' brushes for applying lacquer.

Chamois Leather
Used for protecting metal objects undergoing straightening by applied pressure. Domestic supplier.

Chisel
Used for removing rust concretions from substantial iron objects. Domestic supplier

Cloths
Used for many purposes, such as rags for general mopping up, better quality dusters for general polishing, or impregnated polishing cloths. Domestic or specialist supplier.

Cocktail Stick
Used for fine cleaning on soft metals. Domestic supplier.

Cotton Buds
Used for dabbing on chemicals to specific areas or for fine polishing. Domestic supplier.

Dental Pick
Stainless steel tools used for picking at corrosion products. Specialist supplier.

Dowel
Wooden rods of various diameters useful for applying direct pressure to localised areas i.e. in removing dents. Use with chamois. Domestic supplier.

Drill (hobbyist)
Used for grinding corrosion deposits or localised polishing. Domestic or specialist supplier.

Electrolytic Cleaning Equipment
Used for detaching corrosion products. Specialist supplier.
Emery Paper
Used for coarse polishing. Use finest grade only. Domestic supplier.
Engraving Tool (electrical)
Adapted for mechanical cleaning. Specialist supplier.
Eye Protectors
For use with chemical or mechanical cleaning processes. Domestic or specialist supplier.
Face Mask
For use with chemical or mechanical cleaning processes. Domestic or specialist supplier.
Glass Beakers
For use with chemical processes. Laboratory types have pouring lips, may be calibrated for measuring, and can be heat-resistant. Specialist supplier.
Hammer
Light hammer for use with chisel on iron encrustation. Domestic supplier.
Magnet
Strong magnet used for judging remaining iron under rust coating. Domestic supplier.
Magnifying Glass
Used for fine detail cleaning work and examining surfaces. Table top and hand held types both useful. Domestic supplier.
Measuring Cylinder
Used for accurate measuring of fluid volumes. Specialist supplier.
Needle
Heavy duty sewing needle held in pliers or mounted in home-made handle and used for very fine picking at corrosion. Also adaptable for use in an engraving tool. Domestic supplier.
Plastic Boxes
Domestic food storage types. Useful as chemical baths, and for bulk storage of artefacts. Domestic supplier.
Pliers
Small long-nosed pliers for holding needles, or for straightening bent objects. Domestic supplier.
Pyrex® Pan
Used for heating substances during treatment processes. Domestic supplier.
Scalpel
Used for fine cleaning work. Domestic or specialist supplier.
Surgical Gloves
Used for hand protection. Better fitting than household gloves. Domestic or specialist supplier.

Tongs
Stainless steel crucible type. For holding hot objects, and for placing them in and removing them from chemical solutions. Specialist supplier.
Toothpick
Used for fine cleaning on soft metals. Domestic supplier.
Vice
Small bench mounted or portable type for holding objects steady whilst undergoing treatment. Domestic supplier.
Wire Wool
Used for removing rust from iron.

Appendix 3

Volumes, Weights and Measures

Making Measured Volumes of Chemical Solutions

Follow these procedures to make solutions of the required strengths as outlined in this book. Note that there are two different equations. A solid dissolved in a liquid is measured by a weight to volume ratio (w/v). A liquid diluted with another liquid is measured by a volume to volume ratio (v/v).

Dissolving a solid in a liquid

If 10 grams of solid are dissolved in a small volume of water, which is then increased to 100 millilitres, this will produce a 10% solution as measured by weight to volume*. Therefore a 5% solution is produced by dissolving 5 grams in 100 millilitres. To make a larger volume, increase the amounts in ratio. For example, to make 500 millilitres of 5% EDTA, dissolve 25 grams of EDTA in a little water, then increase the volume to 500 millilitres. You will then have 500 millilitres of 5% w/v EDTA. To make smaller volumes reduce the amounts by ratio.

*Note. If you simply add 10 grams of solid to 100 millilitres of liquid, you will increase the volume of the 100 millilitres by the physical volume of the solid, and in consequence the ratio will not be accurate. The difference however is so slight for the purposes outlined in this book that it need not be of concern.

Diluting one liquid with another

If 10 millilitres of concentrated liquid are diluted with 90 millilitres of distilled water, it will produce a 10% solution. To reduce the strength of a solution previously made up from a solid, increase the volume of solvent by ratio. For example, to make a 5% solution of citric acid from 100 millilitres of a 10% one, add another 100 millilitres of distilled water.

FURTHER READING

Plenderleith H.J. and Werner A.E.A. (1971) *The Conservation of Antiquities and Works of Art,* 2nd edition Oxford University Press.

This book became, and to some extent remains, the conservationists' bible. It covers a wide range of materials as well as metal. Various procedures are outlined in easy to understand terms, with some actual case histories being cited, and the methods that were used described. Although a few treatments have now been superseded by more recent thinking, it remains a very useful handbook.

Cronyn J.M.(1990) *The Elements of Archaeological Conservation.* Routledge

This is another book which also covers the whole spectrum of conservation, and contains more up-to-date information than Plenderleith and Werner. It is perhaps slightly more technical in its content, and a basic understanding of chemistry and physics is an advantage, but for anyone wanting to know what is going on inside their coins or artefacts it is essential reading. It also contains a comprehensive index and bibliography for those interested in pursuing the art of conservation further.